10-STEP GUIDE TO HELP MEN PRESS TOWARDS THE MARK

Copyright © 2024 Frederick A. Quarles Jr.

All rights reserved.

No part of this publication may be reproduced, distributed, or transmitted in any form or by any means, including photocopying, recording, or other electronic, mechanical, or any information storage and retrieval system methods, without the prior written permission of the author.

ISBN:979-8-9905618-0-9

All Scripture quotations, unless otherwise indicated, are taken from the Holy Bible, New International Version®, NIV®. Copyright ©1973, 1978, 1984, 2011 by Biblica, Inc.™ Used by permission of Zondervan. All rights reserved worldwide. www.zondervan.comThe "NIV" and "New International Version" are trademarks registered in the United States Patent and Trademark Office by Biblica, Inc.™

Welcome, gentlemen, to the "10-Step Guide to Help Men Press Towards the Mark." This book is not just another read; it's a call to action, an invitation to embark on a transformative journey of self-discovery, growth, and purpose.

As men, we often find ourselves navigating through the complexities of life, juggling multiple responsibilities, and facing various challenges along the way. Amid this hustle and bustle, it's easy to lose sight of what truly matters and to lose track of the marks we should be pressing towards.

The purpose of this book is simple yet profound: to encourage men like you to identify your mark and press towards it with unwavering determination and faith. But what exactly is this mark we speak of? It's different for each of us, yet it encompasses key areas of our lives where we strive for excellence, fulfillment, and impact.

Throughout the pages of this book, you will be challenged to press towards the marks in TEN crucial areas. Each chapter will focus on one of these areas, presenting a scripture that serves as the foundation for the discussion. We will delve into the scripture, exploring its relevance and application to the topic. You'll find sections for personal reflection, allowing you to pause, ponder, and assess your journey in light of the topic being discussed.

Moreover, sprinkled throughout each chapter, you'll find doses of motivation to keep you going when the going gets tough. Because let's face it, pressing towards the mark isn't always easy. It requires perseverance, resilience, and unwavering determination. But with the right mindset and support, it's a journey that can lead to profound growth and fulfillment.

As you journey through this book, may you be inspired to press toward your mark with renewed vigor and purpose. May you embrace the challenges, celebrate the victories, and strive for excellence in every area of your life. And as you do, may you find strength, wisdom, and guidance in the power of prayer.

Gentlemen! Are you ready to discover and press toward your mark with all your heart, mind, and soul? If so, let's embark on this journey together, one chapter at a time. The mark awaits, and the journey begins now.

MEN:

WHAT IS YOUR MARK?

TABLE OF CONTENTS

Introduction	**7**
Chapter 1: Faith	**11**
Chapter 2: Marriage	**19**
Chapter 3: Fatherhood	**27**
Chapter 4: Family	**37**
Chapter 5: Authentic Relationships	**47**
Chapter 6: Finances	**55**
Chapter 7: Physical Health	**63**
Chapter 8: Career	**71**
Chapter 9: Role Models	**81**
Chapter 10: Legacy	**89**
Conclusion	

ABOUT THE AUTHOR:

Frederick Quarles, the author is from Indianapolis, Indiana. For the past decade, he has been happily married to his wife (Jetaun) and together they have been blessed with four amazing children.

Fred's professional journey has been diverse and impactful, reflecting his passion for empowering others to reach their full potential. He has served in various capacities, including as an Athletic Academic Advisor at the University of Memphis, a Youth Pastor at First Baptist Church-Broad and Church of the Living God, and in several leadership roles at the YMCA, such as Senior

Program Director, Center Director, and Executive Director.

Educationally, Fred holds a Bachelor of Science degree in Business Administration and a Master of Science degree in Recreation and Sports Management. He has also pursued further studies, accumulating 30 hours towards a Master of Divinity degree, and is currently enrolled in a Doctoral program in Philosophy with a specialization in General Psychology, focusing on Performance Psychology.

Aside from his professional pursuits, Fred is deeply passionate about fitness and has actively competed in bodybuilding and powerlifting. However, his greatest joy comes from helping others unleash their potential and achieve their goals. His desire to see men rise to their highest calling fuels his enthusiasm for this book.

Fred aims to inspire and equip men to identify their marks in life and press towards them with courage, determination, and unwavering faith. Through this book, he hopes to empower men to embrace their purpose, strengthen their relationships, and leave a lasting legacy that honors God and impacts the world.

INTRODUCTION

In the pursuit of a fulfilling and purposeful life, men are called to press towards the mark in various aspects of their journey. From matters of faith to family, career to physical health, this book serves as a roadmap for men seeking to navigate life's challenges and achieve their full potential. This book is designed to guide you on this journey toward becoming the man you aspire to be. In a world filled with distractions and competing priorities, it's essential to pause and reflect on what truly matters in life. This book aims to help you do just that.

Each chapter of this book is dedicated to a specific aspect of your life where you can press towards your mark, whether it's in your faith, relationships, health, finances, career, or legacy. By exploring these areas and setting meaningful goals, you can move closer to the man you envision yourself becoming.

Here's what you can expect from each chapter:

- **Chapter 1: Faith** - Explore how to deepen your spiritual connection and live out your faith in practical ways.

- **Chapter 2: Marriage** - Reflect on your relationship with your spouse and learn how to nurture a strong and fulfilling partnership.

- **Chapter 3: Fatherhood** - Consider the impact you have as a father and discover strategies for being the best dad you can be.

- **Chapter 4: Family** - Delve into the importance of family bonds and ways to cultivate a supportive and loving family environment.

- **Chapter 5: Authentic Relationships** - Examine the quality of your friendships and connections with others, striving for authenticity and depth.

- **Chapter 6: Finances** - Take control of your financial future by setting goals and adopting healthy money management habits.

- **Chapter 7: Physical Health** - Prioritize your well-being by focusing on fitness, nutrition, and self-care.

- **Chapter 8: Career** - Define your professional aspirations and develop a plan to achieve success and fulfillment in your career.

- **Chapter 9: Role Models** - Identify positive role models and learn from their examples as you strive to be a source of inspiration to others.

- **Chapter 10: Legacy** - Consider the legacy you want to leave behind and take steps to ensure your life has a lasting impact.

- **Conclusion** - Reflect on your journey and commit to pressing towards your mark with renewed purpose and determination.

Throughout each chapter, you'll find scriptures to meditate on, reflection questions to ponder, practical life applications to implement, real-life examples to inspire and motivate, and a father's prayer for their sons.

I encourage you to approach this book with an open heart and a willingness to embrace growth and change. Remember, the journey towards becoming the man you want to be is not always easy, but it is worth it. So, let's embark on this journey together and press towards the mark of our true potential.

Chapter 1

Faith

"Now faith is confidence in what we hope for and assurance about what we do not see."
Hebrews 11:1

Overview:

In our journey through life as men, faith serves as the bedrock upon which we build our spiritual connection with the divine. Hebrews 11:1 encapsulates the essence of faith as confidence in what we hope for and assurance about what we do not see. In this chapter, we will explore the significance of faith in our lives, how to deepen our spiritual connection, and practical ways to live out our faith.

Hebrews 11:1 serves as a guiding light for men as they press towards the mark in their faith journey.

**Now faith is confidence in what we hope for and assurance about what we do not see.
Hebrews 11:1**

Here's how Hebrews 11:1 helps men to press towards the mark in their faith:

1. **Confidence in Hope:** Men face various challenges and uncertainties in life, but faith provides confidence in the hope of better things. This confidence empowers men to persevere through trials, knowing that God is faithful to fulfill His promises.

2. **Assurance in the Unseen:** Faith enables men to have assurance in the unseen realities of God's kingdom. While we may not see God with our physical eyes, we trust in His presence, His power, and His love. This assurance gives us the courage and perseverance to navigate life's uncertainties.

3. **Steadfastness in Adversity:** Hebrews 11:1 reminds us to remain steadfast in our faith when we encounter obstacles or setbacks. We hold fast to the

hope that God is working all things together for their good, even when circumstances may seem bleak.

4. **Vision for the Future:** Faith provides men with a vision for the future that transcends their current circumstances. It motivates us to press towards the mark, knowing that our ultimate goal is to inherit the promises of God's kingdom.

5. **Active Trust:** True faith is not passive; it requires action. Men are called to actively trust in God's promises, stepping out in obedience even when they cannot see the outcome. This active trust propels us forward in our faith journey, enabling us to overcome obstacles and achieve spiritual growth.

In essence, Hebrews 11:1 inspires men to press toward the mark in their faith by instilling in us a deep sense of confidence, assurance, and perseverance. It serves as a reminder that faith is not just a belief system but a dynamic force that empowers men to live with purpose, passion, and conviction. As men anchor their lives on the promises of God, they are equipped to face life's challenges with unwavering faith and determination.

Reflection Questions:

Take a moment to reflect on your own experiences, beliefs, and aspirations related to your faith. Consider the challenges you've faced, the victories you've celebrated, and the areas where you desire to grow in your relationship with God. Take a moment to answer the questions below:

- What is your mark when it comes to faith?

- What are you pressing towards in your spiritual journey?

Goal Setting:

Setting goals is essential for intentional growth in our faith. Consider specific areas where you want to deepen your spiritual connection and set SMART goals to help you achieve them:

- ✓ **Specific:** Clearly define what you want to accomplish in your faith journey.

- ✓ **Measurable:** Determine how you will measure your progress and success.

- ✓ **Achievable:** Set realistic goals that you can reasonably attain.

- ✓ **Relevant:** Ensure that your goals align with your values and priorities.

- ✓ **Time-bound:** Establish a timeframe for achieving your goals to stay focused and accountable.

Action Steps:

To help you press towards your mark of faith, here are some actionable steps and strategies to consider:

1. **Prioritize Daily Devotions:** Set aside time each day for prayer, meditation, and studying God's word. Use devotionals, Bible reading plans, or journaling to deepen your understanding and connection with God.

2. **Engage in Worship:** Participate in regular worship services, whether in-person or online, to join with other believers in praising and glorifying God. Allow worship to uplift your spirit and draw you closer to Him.

3. **Foster Community:** Surround yourself with a community of believers who can support, encourage, and challenge you in your faith journey. Join a small group, Bible study, or accountability group to grow together in Christ.

4. **Serve Others:** Look for opportunities to serve and minister to those in need, both within your faith community and beyond. Use your gifts, talents, and resources to make a positive impact and reflect the love of Christ to others.

Journaling Space:

Use this blank space to jot down your thoughts, insights, and reflections as you work through your faith goals. Record moments of spiritual growth, answered prayers, and challenges faced. Your journal will serve as a valuable tool for tracking your progress and deepening your relationship with God.

Conclusion:

As we conclude this chapter, let us lift a prayer for all men who are pressing toward their faith:

Heavenly Father, we thank you for the gift of faith and the opportunity to grow closer to you each day. Grant us the strength, wisdom, and courage to live out our faith boldly and authentically. May our hearts be filled with confidence in your promises, and may we walk in assurance of your presence with us always. In Jesus name, Amen.

Chapter 2
Marriage: Nurturing a Strong and Fulfilling Partnership

"Husbands love their wives, just as Christ loved the church and gave himself up for her."
Ephesians 5:25 (NIV)

Overview:

Marriage is a sacred institution ordained by God, designed to be a source of love, companionship, and mutual support. In this chapter, we will delve into the profound responsibility and privilege that men have in nurturing a strong and fulfilling partnership with their spouses. Drawing upon the timeless wisdom of Ephesians 5:25, we will explore the selfless love, sacrificial commitment, and servant leadership that characterize a Christ-centered marriage.

"Ephesians 5:25 (NIV): Husbands, love your wives, just as Christ loved the church and gave himself up for her."

This verse provides a profound insight into the sacrificial love that husbands are called to demonstrate towards their wives, mirroring the selfless love that Christ has for His church. Here's how Ephesians 5:25 encourages men to press towards the mark in their marriages:

1. **Selfless Love:** Just as Christ loved the church and gave Himself up for her, men are called to love their wives selflessly. This entails putting their wives' needs above their own, prioritizing their well-being, and making sacrifices for their happiness and fulfillment.

2. **Commitment:** The act of giving oneself up for one's spouse implies a deep commitment to the marriage covenant. Men are encouraged to remain steadfast and unwavering in their commitment to their wives, regardless of the challenges or trials they may face.

3. **Servant Leadership:** Christ's love for the church is characterized by servant leadership, and husbands are called to emulate this example in their marriages. They are tasked with leading their families with humility, compassion, and a servant's heart, seeking their wives' best interests above their own.

4. **Nurturing and Cherishing:** Just as Christ nurtures and cherishes the church; husbands are called to nurture and cherish their wives. This involves providing emotional support, encouragement, and affirmation, as well as creating a safe and loving environment where their wives can flourish and grow.

5. **Protecting and Providing:** Christ's love is protective and provides for the needs of His church, and husbands are called to likewise protect and provide for their wives. This includes not only physical protection and provision but also emotional support, spiritual guidance, and relational security.

In summary, Ephesians 5:25 underscores the profound responsibility and privilege that men have in their marriages. By loving their wives sacrificially, committing to their marriage covenant, leading with humility, nurturing and cherishing their spouses, and providing and protecting their families, men can press towards the mark in their marriages and cultivate relationships that reflect the love and grace of Christ.

Reflection Questions:
Reflect on your own experiences, beliefs, and aspirations related to marriage. Consider the areas where you may need to grow and improve as a husband. Take a moment to answer the questions below:

As men, what mark are we pressing towards in our marriages?

How can we cultivate deeper intimacy, understanding, and connection with our spouses?

Practical Life Applications:

Apply the principles of selfless love, sacrificial commitment, and servant leadership to your daily interactions with your spouse. Practice humility, patience, and grace in navigating challenges and conflicts in your marriage. Seek opportunities to serve and support your partner, demonstrating Christ-like love in every aspect of your relationship.

Real-Life Examples:

Draw inspiration from real-life examples of couples who have cultivated thriving marriages rooted in faith, love, and mutual respect. Learn from their experiences, challenges, and triumphs, and glean valuable insights that you can apply to your relationship.

Goal Setting:

Set specific, measurable, achievable, relevant, and time-bound (SMART) goals related to pressing toward a stronger marriage. Identify areas where you can enhance communication, deepen emotional intimacy, and prioritize quality time with your spouse. Determine actionable steps to address any challenges or conflicts that may be hindering the health of your relationship.

Action Steps:
- Implement practical strategies to strengthen your marriage and fulfill your role as a husband.

- Practice active listening, empathy, and forgiveness in your interactions with your spouse.

- Make intentional efforts to express love, appreciation, and admiration for your partner daily.

- Prioritize quality time together, whether through date nights, shared hobbies, or meaningful conversations.

Journaling Space:

Use the blank pages provided to jot down your thoughts, insights, and progress as you work through the workbook. Reflect on the lessons learned from Ephesians 5:25 and how they apply to your marriage. Take note of any areas where you see growth and improvement, as well as areas where you may need to seek further guidance or support.

Conclusion:
As we conclude this chapter, let us lift our marriages in prayer, seeking God's guidance, strength, and blessing upon our unions.

May we continue to press towards the mark in our marriages, striving to love and honor our spouses as Christ loves the church.
In Jesus name, Amen.

Chapter 3

Fatherhood - Embracing the Role of a Father

"These commandments that I give you today are to be on your hearts. Impress them on your children. Talk about them when you sit at home and when you walk along the road when you lie down, and when you get up."
Deuteronomy 6:6-7 (NIV)

Overview:
Fatherhood is a sacred responsibility, a calling that carries profound significance in shaping the lives of our children and leaving a lasting impact on future generations. In this chapter, we will delve into the essential aspects of fatherhood, exploring how we can fulfill our role as fathers with purpose, intentionality, and love. Grounded in the timeless wisdom of Deuteronomy 6:6-7, we will uncover strategies for being the best dads we can be,

nurturing our children's spiritual, emotional, and physical well-being.

Deuteronomy 6:6-7 is a powerful scripture that emphasizes the role of fathers in nurturing their children spiritually and guiding them towards a life of faith. Here's the passage:

"These commandments that I give you today are to be on your hearts. Impress them on your children. Talk about them when you sit at home and when you walk along the road when you lie down, and when you get up."

Deuteronomy 6:6-7 (NIV)

This scripture underscores the importance of fathers instilling God's commandments and teachings in the hearts of their children through consistent and intentional instruction. It encourages fathers to integrate spiritual conversations and lessons into every aspect of their daily lives, whether at home, on the go, or during moments of rest.

For men pressing towards the mark as fathers, Deuteronomy 6:6-7 serves as a guiding principle, reminding them of their responsibility to actively engage in their children's spiritual upbringing. Fathers should model a life of faith, and nurture their children's relationship with God through regular teaching, conversation, and example.

Deuteronomy 6:6-7 provides invaluable guidance for fathers as they press towards the mark in their roles within the family. Let's explore how this scripture helps fathers:

1. **Importance of Spiritual Education:** Deuteronomy 6:6-7 emphasizes the importance of imparting spiritual education to children. Fathers are instructed to impress God's commandments upon their children, teaching them diligently. This underscores the critical role fathers play in shaping their children's spiritual growth and understanding. By prioritizing spiritual education, fathers can help their children develop a strong foundation of faith, enabling them to navigate life's challenges with wisdom and discernment.

2. **Integration of Faith into Daily Life:** The scripture instructs fathers to talk about God's commandments with their children in various contexts—whether at home, on the road, before sleeping, or upon waking up. This highlights the importance of integrating faith into every aspect of family life. Fathers are encouraged to seize everyday opportunities to discuss and demonstrate God's principles, fostering a culture of faith that permeates their family's interactions and routines.

3. **Modeling Authentic Faith:** Children often learn by example, and Deuteronomy 6:6-7 underscores the significance of fathers modeling authentic faith. As fathers live out their relationship with God, they provide a tangible example for their children to follow. By demonstrating devotion, obedience, and trust in God, fathers inspire their children to embrace a similar faith journey. Thus, fathers play a pivotal role in shaping their children's spiritual identity through their commitment to pressing toward the mark of authentic faith.

4. **Building Strong Family Bonds:** Engaging in regular discussions about faith and God's commandments fosters deeper connections within the family. Fathers who prioritize spiritual conversations create opportunities for meaningful dialogue, bonding, and mutual understanding among family members. Through shared experiences of learning and growing in faith together, fathers strengthen the familial bond, nurturing a supportive and loving environment where every member feels valued and supported.

5. **Ensuring Generational Legacy:** By faithfully following the instructions outlined in Deuteronomy 6:6-7, fathers contribute to the continuity of God's covenant across generations. As they pass down spiritual knowledge and values to their children, fathers play a vital role in ensuring the preservation of faith within their family lineage. Through intentional efforts to press towards the mark as spiritual leaders, fathers leave a lasting legacy of faithfulness and devotion that extends beyond their lifetimes.

In summary, Deuteronomy 6:6-7 serves as a guiding principle for fathers as they press towards the mark in their roles within the family. It highlights the importance of spiritual education, the integration of faith into daily life, modeling authentic faith, building strong family bonds, and ensuring a generational legacy of faithfulness. As fathers embrace these principles, they empower their children to grow in their relationship with God, laying a foundation for a thriving and spiritually grounded family unit.

<u>Reflection Questions:</u>
As we embark on this journey of exploring fatherhood, let's take a moment to reflect on our own experiences, beliefs, and aspirations related to this crucial aspect of our lives. Take a moment to answer the questions below:

- What does fatherhood mean to you?

- How do you envision your role as a father impacting your children's lives?

- What are some of the challenges you face as a father, and how do you navigate them?

Real-Life Examples:

Drawing inspiration from real-life stories of fathers who have embraced their role with dedication and devotion can motivate and encourage us on our journey. Let's explore stories of fathers who have made a positive impact on their children's lives through their love, guidance, and support.

Goal Setting:

Setting specific, measurable, achievable, relevant, and time-bound (SMART) goals related to fatherhood can help us stay focused and intentional in our journey as dads.

Let's consider setting goals such as:

✓ Spending quality time with each child individually regularly.

✓ Being more present and engaged during family meals and activities.

✓ Setting aside dedicated time for spiritual guidance and mentorship.

<u>Action Steps:</u>
Taking tangible actions toward achieving our goals is essential for making meaningful progress in our journey as fathers. Here are some actionable steps we can take:

- Schedule regular father-child outings or activities to strengthen our bond with each child.

- Create a family routine that includes designated times for shared meals, conversations, and spiritual reflections.

- Seek out resources and support networks for fathers, such as parenting classes or mentorship programs

Journaling Space:

Use this space to jot down your thoughts, insights, and progress. Reflect on your experiences, challenges, and successes as a father, and consider how you can continue to grow and evolve in this vital role.

Conclusion:
As we conclude this chapter, let's commit to embracing our role as fathers with courage, compassion, and conviction. Let's press towards the mark of fatherhood, striving to be the best dads we can be and leaving a legacy of love and wisdom for generations to come. May we always seek guidance and strength from above as we navigate the joys and challenges of fatherhood.

Heavenly Father, we thank you for the gift of fatherhood and the privilege of shaping the lives of our children. Grant us wisdom, patience, and love as we fulfill our role as fathers. Help us to lead by example, instilling in our children the values of faith, integrity, and compassion. Guide us in our journey of fatherhood, and may your grace sustain us every step of the way.
In Jesus' name, amen.

Chapter 4

Family - Cultivating a Strong and Loving Family Environment

"But if serving the Lord seems undesirable to you, then choose for yourselves this day whom you will serve, whether the gods your ancestors served beyond the Euphrates, or the gods of the Amorites, in whose land you are living. But as for me and my household, we will serve the Lord."
Joshua 24:15 (NIV)

Overview:

Family is the cornerstone of society, the foundation upon which we build our lives and relationships. In this chapter, we will delve into the importance of family bonds and explore ways to nurture a supportive and loving family environment. Drawing inspiration from the timeless wisdom of Joshua 24:15, we will learn how to prioritize serving the

Lord within our households and guide our families toward a life of faith and unity.

But if serving the Lord seems undesirable to you, then choose for yourselves this day whom you will serve, whether the gods your ancestors served beyond the Euphrates, or the gods of the Amorites, in whose land you are living. But as for me and my household, we will serve the Lord."
Joshua 24:15 (NIV)

Joshua 24:15 serves as a powerful reminder of the importance of intentional spiritual leadership within our families. In this verse, Joshua declares, "But as for me and my household, we will serve the Lord." This statement encapsulates Joshua's unwavering commitment to prioritize serving God within his own family, setting a powerful example for us to follow.

This scripture highlights the importance of spiritual leadership within the family unit. It emphasizes the father's role in setting the tone for faithfulness and devotion to God within the household. By choosing to serve the Lord and lead his family in righteousness, a man demonstrates his commitment to nurturing a godly heritage and guiding his loved ones toward a life of faith.

Joshua 24:15 encourages men to prioritize their family's spiritual well-being and actively lead them in pursuing God's purposes. It underscores the significance of making intentional decisions to honor God and instill His principles in the family's daily life, fostering a legacy of faithfulness and devotion for generations to come.

Here's how Joshua 24:15 helps men press towards the mark in their families:

1. **Clarifies Priorities:** By declaring his family's commitment to serving the Lord, Joshua emphasizes the importance of spiritual values and priorities within the family unit. This verse challenges us to consider what values we want to instill in our families and to make a deliberate choice to prioritize serving God above all else.

2. **Provides Leadership:** Joshua's declaration demonstrates strong leadership within the family. As men, we are called to lead our households in righteousness, guiding our families toward a life of faith and obedience to God's commands. Joshua's example inspires us to take on the role of spiritual leaders within our own families, guiding and nurturing our loved ones in their journey of faith.

3. **Encourages Commitment:** Joshua's resolute declaration reflects a deep-seated commitment to God and His ways. Similarly, men are encouraged to make a firm commitment to serving the Lord within their families, even in the face of challenges or opposition. This commitment serves as a guiding principle that shapes every aspect of family life, from decision-making to daily interactions.

4. **Promotes Unity:** Joshua's words foster unity within the family unit. By declaring a shared commitment to serve the Lord, Joshua unites his household under a common purpose and vision. Likewise, men are called to cultivate unity within their families, fostering an environment of mutual

love, respect, and cooperation as they press towards the mark together.

5. **Inspires Action:** Finally, Joshua 24:15 inspires action. It challenges men to actively engage in spiritual leadership within their families, taking deliberate steps to cultivate a household that honors and serves the Lord. Whether through regular family devotions, intentional conversations about faith, or modeling Christ-like behavior, men are called to put their faith into action within their families.

In summary, Joshua 24:15 serves as a guiding light for men as they press toward the mark in their families. It inspires us to prioritize serving God, provides a model of strong leadership, encourages commitment and unity, and motivates us to take tangible actions to nurture a household that honors God in all things.

Reflection Questions:
As you reflect on your own experiences and beliefs regarding family, consider the following questions:

What values and principles do you want to instill in your family?

How do you currently prioritize serving the Lord within your household?

What steps can you take to strengthen the bonds within your family and cultivate a loving environment?

Goal Setting:
Setting specific, measurable goals is essential for pressing towards the mark in your family life. Consider setting goals such as:

- ✓ Committing to regular family devotional time or prayer sessions.

- ✓ Planning and scheduling quality family time activities.

- ✓ Establishing open communication channels to foster understanding and unity.

Action Steps:

Taking tangible actions is key to implementing positive changes within your family dynamic.

Consider the following action steps:

- Schedule regular family meetings to discuss goals, concerns, and plans.

- Create a family mission statement outlining your shared values and goals.

- Prioritize spending quality time together, whether through shared meals, outings, or bonding activities.

Journaling Space:

Use the space provided to jot down your thoughts, insights, and reflections as you work through the workbook. Take note of any significant moments or breakthroughs in your journey toward cultivating a strong and loving family environment.

Conclusion:

As we conclude this chapter, let us reaffirm our commitment to serving the Lord within our households and nurturing a supportive and loving family environment. May our efforts be guided by the timeless wisdom of Joshua 24:15, as we strive to press towards the mark in our family life. Let us pray for wisdom, strength, and grace as we lead our families in faith and unity.

Chapter 5

Authentic Relationships

"As iron sharpens iron, so one person sharpens another."
Proverbs 27:17

Overview:

As you embark on this journey of pressing toward authentic relationships, may you experience the joy and fulfillment that comes from connecting deeply with others and sharpening one another in love. Authentic relationships are essential for personal growth, support, and fulfillment. In this chapter, we will delve into the significance of cultivating genuine connections with others and explore practical ways to strengthen the quality of your friendships and relationships. Drawing inspiration from Proverbs 27:17, we will uncover the transformative power of mutual sharpening and encouragement in authentic relationships.

Proverbs 27:17 (NIV), states: "As iron sharpens iron, so one person sharpens another."

This scripture emphasizes the significance of genuine, supportive relationships in a man's life. Here's how it relates to men pressing toward the mark in developing authentic relationships:

1. Mutual Growth: Just as iron sharpens iron, authentic relationships enable mutual growth and development. Men need companions who challenge, encourage, and uplift them as they strive to become their best selves. By surrounding themselves with individuals who sharpen them intellectually, emotionally, and spiritually, men can continually press toward their mark of personal growth and excellence.

2. Accountability: Authentic relationships provide a foundation of accountability, where men hold each other to high standards of character and integrity. Through honest feedback, constructive criticism, and mutual support, men in genuine relationships help each other stay accountable to their goals and values. This accountability fosters personal growth and empowers men to overcome obstacles on their journey toward the mark.

3. Emotional Support: In authentic relationships, men find a safe space to express their emotions, vulnerabilities, and struggles. These connections offer empathetic listening, understanding, and emotional support, which are essential for navigating life's challenges. By cultivating authentic relationships built on trust and empathy, men can find solace, encouragement, and companionship as they press toward their mark, knowing they are not alone in their journey.

4. Shared Values: Authentic relationships are grounded in shared values, beliefs, and interests. Men who develop meaningful connections with others who share their core values experience a sense of camaraderie and solidarity. These relationships provide a sense of belonging and affirmation, reinforcing men's commitment to their mark and fostering a supportive community of like-minded individuals.

5. Fulfillment and Joy: Genuine relationships bring fulfillment, joy, and richness to men's lives. Through meaningful connections with others, men experience a deeper sense of purpose, belonging, and happiness. As they press toward their mark in the context of authentic relationships, men find encouragement, companionship, and shared experiences that enrich their journey and enhance their overall well-being.

In essence, Proverbs 27:17 underscores the transformative power of authentic relationships in men's lives. By surrounding themselves with supportive companions who sharpen, challenge, and uplift them, men can press toward their mark with greater resilience, accountability, and fulfillment. These genuine connections provide a source of strength, encouragement, and companionship that propel men forward on their journey of personal growth and excellence.

Reflection Questions:
1. What is your mark when it comes to cultivating authentic relationships?

2. How do your current friendships and connections contribute to your growth and well-being?
3. In what ways can you deepen the authenticity and depth of your relationships with others?

Goal Setting:
- ✓ Identify specific qualities you value in authentic relationships, such as honesty, vulnerability, and mutual respect.

- ✓ Set goals for nurturing existing friendships and forming new connections based on these values.

- ✓ Determine actionable steps to enhance communication, trust, and intimacy in your relationships

Action Steps:
- Initiate open and honest conversations with friends about your desire for deeper connections.

- Practice active listening and empathy to better understand the experiences and perspectives of others.

- Be intentional about spending quality time with loved ones and investing in meaningful interactions.

- Seek opportunities to support and encourage others in their personal and spiritual growth journeys.

- Foster a culture of authenticity and vulnerability within your social circles by leading by example.

Journaling Space:

Reflect on your recent interactions and experiences with friends and loved ones.

- What insights have you gained about the nature of your relationships?

- How can you apply the principles of authenticity and mutual sharpening in your interactions moving forward?

Heavenly Father, thank you for the gift of relationships that enrich our lives and strengthen our faith. Help us to cultivate authentic connections with others, rooted in love, grace, and mutual support. Guide us in being intentional about nurturing meaningful friendships and being sources of encouragement and inspiration to those around us. May our relationships reflect your goodness and bring glory to your name. In Jesus name, Amen.

Chapter 6

Finances - Taking Control of Your Financial Future

"The wise store up choice food and olive oil, but fools gulp theirs down."
Proverbs 21:20

Overview:

In this chapter, we delve into the realm of finances, exploring how men can take control of their financial future by setting goals and adopting healthy money management habits. Drawing inspiration from Proverbs 21:20, we learn valuable lessons about the importance of wisdom and prudence in financial matters.

This verse emphasizes the importance of wise financial management and planning for the future. It encourages men to be intentional and disciplined in their financial decisions, prioritizing savings and investments over impulsive spending. By applying the wisdom found in Proverbs 21:20, men can cultivate financial stewardship, prudently manage their resources, and work towards achieving their financial goals.

> "The wise store up choice food and olive oil, but fools gulp theirs down."
> **Proverbs 21:20**

Proverbs 21:20 offers valuable insights for men seeking to press towards the mark in their finances. Here's how this scripture can guide them:

1. Wisdom in Financial Management: The verse highlights the contrast between the wise and the foolish in their approach to resources. Men are encouraged to adopt the wisdom of storing up provisions, such as food and oil, for future needs. This suggests the importance of budgeting, saving, and planning for financial stability.

2. Long-Term Perspective: By storing up choice food and oil, individuals demonstrate foresight and consideration for the future. Likewise, men are urged to take a long-term view of their finances, making decisions that benefit them not only in the present but also in the years to come. This may involve setting financial goals, prioritizing savings, and investing wisely.

3. Avoiding Impulsiveness: The contrast between storing up provisions and gulping them down underscores the danger of impulsive spending and short-sightedness. Men are reminded to resist the temptation to consume everything immediately and instead exercise self-control and prudence in their financial habits.

4. Building Financial Security: By following the wisdom of Proverbs 21:20, men can work towards building financial security and resilience. By saving and investing wisely, they lay the foundation for stability, preparedness for emergencies, and the ability to weather economic challenges.

In summary, Proverbs 21:20 encourages men to approach their finances with wisdom, foresight, and self-discipline, guiding them toward prudent financial management and the pursuit of long-term prosperity.

Reflection Questions:

1. What is your mark when it comes to finances?

2. What financial goals are you pressing towards?

3. How do your current financial habits align with the principles of wisdom outlined in Proverbs 21:20?

Goal Setting:

- ✓ **Identify your financial goals:** Take time to define your short-term and long-term financial objectives, such as saving for emergencies, paying off debt, investing for retirement, or purchasing a home.

- ✓ **Make your goals SMART:** Ensure that your financial goals are Specific, Measurable, Achievable, Relevant, and Time-bound.

✓ **Develop an action plan:** Break down each goal into smaller, actionable steps that you can take to move closer to financial success.

Action Steps:
- **Create a budget:** Establish a budget that outlines your income, expenses, and savings goals. Track your spending to ensure that you are living within your means and allocating resources wisely.

- **Save consistently:** Prioritize saving by setting aside a portion of your income each month. Consider automating your savings to ensure consistency and discipline.

- **Invest wisely:** Educate yourself about different investment options and strategies. Seek professional advice if needed and diversify your investment portfolio to mitigate risk.

- **Avoid debt:** Be cautious about taking on unnecessary debt and strive to pay off existing debts as soon as possible. Practice responsible borrowing and avoid living beyond your means.

Journaling Space:

Reflect on your current financial situation and your progress toward your financial goals. Use this space to jot down insights, challenges, and achievements related to your financial journey.

As you embark on your journey towards financial stability and prosperity, may you be guided by the wisdom of Proverbs 21:20. May you cultivate habits of prudence, discipline, and stewardship, allowing you to build a solid foundation for your financial future. Let us conclude this chapter with a prayer, seeking God's guidance and blessing as we press toward our financial goals.

Heavenly Father, we ask for Your wisdom and guidance as we strive to take control of our financial futures. Help us to be diligent and faithful stewards of the blessings You have given us. Grant us the discipline to manage our finances wisely, to save prudently, and to give generously. We commit our financial goals and plans to You, believing that with Your help, we can achieve a secure and prosperous future. May our financial success be a testimony to Your faithfulness and a means to bless others. In Jesus' name, we pray, Amen.

Chapter 7
Physical Health - Honoring Your Body as a Temple

"Do you not know that your bodies are temples of the Holy Spirit, who is in you, whom you have received from God? You are not your own; you were bought at a price. Therefore, honor God with your bodies."
1 Corinthians 6:19-20 (NIV)

Overview:

In this chapter, we will explore the significance of prioritizing physical health and well-being as men. Drawing inspiration from the scriptural foundation provided in 1 Corinthians 6:19-20, we will delve into the idea of our bodies being temples of the Holy Spirit, entrusted to us by God. Our bodies are sacred vessels entrusted to us by God, and it is our responsibility to care for them. We will delve into the significance of treating our bodies as temples of the Holy Spirit and the impact that honoring God with our bodies can have on our overall health and lifestyle. Through reflection, goal setting, actionable steps, and prayer, we will embark on a journey to honor God with our bodies by pursuing fitness, proper nutrition, and self-care.

> "Do you not know that your bodies are temples of the Holy Spirit, who is in you, whom you have received from God? You are not your own; you were bought at a price. Therefore, honor God with your bodies."
> **1 Corinthians 6:19-20 (NIV)**

1 Corinthians 6:19-20 serves as a powerful reminder for men to prioritize their physical health and well-being. This scripture emphasizes the sacredness of our bodies as temples of the Holy Spirit, highlighting the divine presence within us. Here's how this scripture helps men press towards the mark in their physical health:

1. **Understanding the Value of the Body:** The scripture reminds men that their bodies are not their own but are temples of the Holy Spirit. This

understanding instills a sense of reverence and respect for the body, recognizing it as a precious gift from God.

2. Responsibility for Self-Care: By acknowledging that we were bought at a price, men are reminded of their responsibility to care for their bodies. This includes adopting healthy lifestyle habits such as regular exercise, balanced nutrition, adequate rest, and avoiding harmful behaviors like substance abuse.

3. Honoring God with our Bodies: The scripture calls men to honor God with their bodies. This means taking proactive steps to maintain good physical health, not only for personal well-being but also as an act of worship and obedience to God.

4. Motivation for Change: Understanding that the Holy Spirit dwells within us can serve as a motivating factor for men to prioritize their physical health. Knowing that our bodies serve as vessels for God's presence can inspire men to make positive changes in their lifestyle habits and choices.

5. Stewardship Mentality: Viewing our bodies as temples of the Holy Spirit encourages men to adopt a stewardship mentality towards their health. This involves being intentional about caring for the body, ensuring its proper maintenance and upkeep to fulfill its purpose in serving God's kingdom.

Overall, 1 Corinthians 6:19-20 reminds men of the spiritual significance of their physical bodies and encourages them to honor God by prioritizing their health and well-being. By embracing this scripture, men can cultivate a holistic approach to fitness, nutrition, and self-care, ultimately pressing toward the mark of optimal physical health and vitality.

Reflection Questions:

1. What is your mark when it comes to physical health?

2. How do you currently prioritize your well-being?

3. In what ways do you feel called to improve your physical health?

Goal Setting:

✓ Set specific fitness goals for yourself, such as weight loss, muscle gain, or cardiovascular endurance.

✓ Establish a nutrition plan that aligns with your health and fitness goals, focusing on wholesome, nourishing foods.

✓ Create a self-care routine that includes activities to promote mental and emotional well-being, such as meditation, journaling, or spending time in nature.

Action Steps:

- Incorporate regular exercise into your weekly schedule, aiming for at least 30 minutes of physical activity most days of the week.

- Make mindful food choices that fuel your body with nutrients and support your overall health and vitality.

- Prioritize adequate sleep, hydration, and stress management to optimize your physical well-being.

- Seek support from a healthcare professional, personal trainer, or nutritionist if needed to help you reach your goals.

Journaling Space:

Take some time to reflect on your current habits and behaviors related to physical health. Write down any insights or revelations that come to mind, as well as your action plan for moving forward.

Conclusion:

As men, it is our responsibility to steward our bodies well and honor God with our physical health. By aligning our actions with the truth of 1 Corinthians 6:19-20, we can cultivate habits that promote vitality, strength, and longevity. Let us commit to pressing towards the mark in our physical health, recognizing that our bodies are temples of the Holy Spirit, deserving of care, respect, and reverence. May our journey towards greater well-being bring glory to God and inspire others to do the same.

Heavenly Father, we thank you for the gift of our bodies and the opportunity to honor you with our physical health. Help us to prioritize our well-being and make choices that reflect our commitment to serving you. Guide us as we set goals, take action steps, and seek to improve our overall fitness and vitality. May our efforts bring glory to your name. In Jesus name, Amen.

Chapter 8

Career - Pressing Towards Your Professional Purpose

"Whatever you do, work at it with all your heart, as working for the Lord, not for human masters, since you know that you will receive an inheritance from the Lord as a reward. It is the Lord Christ you are serving."
Colossians 3:23-24 (NIV)

Overview:

In this chapter, we will delve into the realm of career and vocational aspirations, exploring how men can define their professional goals and develop a plan to achieve success and fulfillment in their chosen paths. Drawing inspiration from Colossians 3:23-24, we will learn how to approach our work with diligence, integrity, and a sense of purpose, recognizing that our ultimate service is to the Lord.

Colossians 3:23-24 provides a powerful exhortation to Christians regarding their approach to work and service:

"Whatever you do, work at it with all your heart, as working for the Lord, not for human masters, since you know that you will receive an inheritance from the Lord as a reward. It is the Lord Christ you are serving."
Colossians 3:23-24 (NIV)

Work at it with all your heart: encourages wholehearted devotion and commitment in whatever task or responsibility one undertakes. It speaks to the importance of giving one's best effort and energy to the work at hand. Working for the Lord: shifts the focus from earthly masters or employers to a higher authority—God Himself. It underscores the idea that all work should be done with the awareness that it is ultimately done for God's glory and honor.

This scripture provides several insights that can guide men in their careers:

1. Work with Excellence: The verse encourages men to approach their work with diligence and excellence, regardless of their occupation or position. By doing so, they honor God and demonstrate integrity in their professional endeavors.

2. Serve God: The scripture emphasizes that men should view their work as a means of serving the Lord rather than merely serving human supervisors or employers. This perspective shifts the focus from seeking approval or recognition from people to seeking fulfillment and purpose in serving God through their work.

3. Motivation for Success: Knowing that their ultimate reward comes from the Lord serves as a powerful motivation for men to excel in their careers. It reminds them that their efforts and contributions are not in vain and that their work has eternal significance beyond worldly achievements.

4. Steadfastness in Adversity: Believing in the promise of an inheritance from the Lord can provide men with the strength and perseverance to navigate challenges and setbacks in their careers. It encourages them to remain steadfast in their faith and commitment, trusting in God's provision and guidance.

5. Alignment with God's Will: By working with the mindset of serving the Lord, men can seek alignment with God's will in their career choices and decisions. This involves seeking God's guidance, prioritizing values consistent with His teachings, and being open to His leading in their vocational journey.

Overall, Colossians 3:23-24 underscores the importance of integrating faith into the workplace and encourages men to pursue their careers with purpose, passion, and dedication, ultimately pressing towards the mark of fulfilling God's calling in their professional lives.

Reflection Questions:

1. What are your current career aspirations, and how do they align with your values and beliefs?

2. How do you approach your work daily? Do you view it as a means of serving the Lord?

3. What obstacles or challenges do you face in pursuing your professional goals, and how can you overcome them?

4. How can you leverage your skills, talents, and passions to make a meaningful impact in your career field?

5. In what ways can you honor God with your work and strive for excellence in your professional endeavors?

Goal Setting:
- ✓ **Define Your Professional Vision:** Take time to clarify your long-term career goals and aspirations, identifying the specific outcomes you hope to achieve.

- ✓ **Set SMART Goals**: Break down your overarching career vision into smaller, measurable objectives that are Specific, Measurable, Achievable, Relevant, and Time-bound.

- ✓ **Create an Action Plan**: Outline the steps you need to take to progress towards your career goals, setting deadlines and milestones to track your progress.

- ✓ **Seek Mentorship and Guidance**: Identify mentors or role models who can provide valuable insights and support as you navigate your career journey.

- ✓ **Continuously Evaluate and Adjust**: Regularly review your goals and progress, making adjustments as needed to stay aligned with your evolving aspirations and circumstances.

Action Steps:

- **Invest in Continuous Learning:** Commit to ongoing personal and professional development, seeking opportunities to expand your skills, knowledge, and expertise.

- **Build Your Network:** Cultivate relationships with colleagues, industry peers, and mentors who can offer guidance, support, and opportunities for growth.

- **Pursue Excellence:** Approach your work with a spirit of excellence, striving to deliver high-quality results and exceed expectations in everything you do.

- **Take Calculated Risks:** Don't be afraid to step out of your comfort zone and pursue new opportunities or challenges that can propel your career forward.

- **Prioritize Work-Life Balance:** Maintain a healthy balance between your professional and personal life, prioritizing self-care, relationships, and well-being.

Journaling Space:

Reflect on your career aspirations, jotting down any insights, challenges, or action steps that arise during your contemplation. Use this space to track your progress and celebrate your achievements as you press towards your professional purpose.

Conclusion:
As we conclude this chapter, let us offer a prayer for guidance, wisdom, and strength as we navigate our career paths. May we honor God with our work, serve others with humility and integrity, and pursue our professional goals with passion and purpose. Amen.

Chapter 9

Role Models - Becoming a Beacon of Inspiration

"Don't let anyone look down on you because you are young, but set an example for the believers in speech, in conduct, in love, in faith and purity."
1 Timothy 4:12

Overview:

In this chapter, we will explore the profound impact of positive role models and the vital role they play in shaping our lives. Drawing inspiration from 1 Timothy 4:12, we will delve into what it means to be a role model and how we can embody qualities that uplift and inspire others. By examining the characteristics outlined in the scripture, we will uncover actionable strategies for becoming exemplary role models in speech, conduct, love, faith, and purity.

1 Timothy 4:12 (NIV):
"Don't let anyone look down on you because you are young, but set an example for the believers in speech, in conduct, in love, in faith and purity."

This verse encourages men, regardless of their age, to be exemplary in various aspects of their lives, serving as positive role models for others. It emphasizes the importance of integrity in speech, behavior, love, faith, and moral purity. As role models, men are called to lead by example, inspiring and guiding others through their actions and character.

1 Timothy 4:12 encourages men to press towards the mark as role models by providing them with a clear directive on how to conduct themselves in a manner worthy of emulation. Here's how this scripture helps men in this regard:

1. Setting an Example: The verse begins by advising men not to let anyone look down on them because of their age. This implies that regardless of age or life stage, men can set an example for others.

It empowers us to embrace our influence and recognize our potential impact on those around us.

2. In Speech: Men are encouraged to be mindful of their words, using speech that is uplifting, truthful, and edifying. This means refraining from gossip, negativity, or any form of communication that may bring others down. Instead, we should strive to speak words of encouragement, wisdom, and grace.

3. In Conduct: The scripture emphasizes the importance of behavior that aligns with our values and beliefs. Men are called to live lives of integrity, demonstrating honesty, kindness, and respect in their interactions with others. We become role models worth following by exhibiting ethical behavior and making morally sound choices.

4. In Love: Men are urged to express love in their actions and relationships. This entails showing compassion, empathy, and generosity towards others, regardless of differences or disagreements. By cultivating a spirit of love and goodwill, we can positively impact those around us and foster a sense of unity and harmony.

5. In Faith: Faithfulness is highlighted as a key characteristic of effective role models. Men are encouraged to demonstrate unwavering faith in God and trust in His guidance and provision. This involves living out our beliefs with conviction and relying on God's strength to navigate life's challenges with courage and perseverance.

6. In Purity: The scripture underscores the importance of moral purity in all aspects of life. Men are called to maintain purity of heart, mind, and body, avoiding harmful influences and behaviors that compromise their integrity. By upholding moral standards and striving for holiness, we can inspire others to pursue righteousness and live lives of honor.

Overall, 1 Timothy 4:12 serves as a roadmap for men to follow as they strive to press toward the mark as role models. It reminds us of our responsibility to lead by example, embodying virtues such as integrity, love, faith, and purity in our everyday lives. By embracing these principles, men can positively influence others and leave a lasting legacy of righteousness and godliness.

Reflection Questions:
1. What qualities do you admire most in the role models you look up to?

2. How do you currently embody the characteristics of a positive role model in your own life?

3. In what areas do you feel you could improve as a role model for others?

Goal Setting:
- ✓ Identify three specific areas where you aim to enhance your role-modeling abilities.

- ✓ Set SMART goals for each area, outlining measurable steps to achieve them.

- ✓ Commit to a timeline for achieving these goals, holding yourself accountable to your aspirations.

Action Steps:

- Practice mindful speech by choosing words that uplift and encourage others.

- Lead by example in your conduct, demonstrating integrity, kindness, and humility.

- Cultivate a spirit of love by showing compassion, empathy, and generosity towards others.

- Strengthen your faith through regular spiritual practices such as prayer, meditation, and scripture study.

- Maintain purity in your thoughts, actions, and relationships, honoring God with your body and mind.

Journaling Space:

Reflect on your progress in becoming a role model in each of the five areas outlined in 1 Timothy 4:12. Consider moments where you have successfully embodied these qualities and areas where you can still grow. Use this space to record your thoughts, insights, and observations as you continue on your journey of personal and spiritual development.

As you engage with the content of this chapter, may you be inspired to embrace your role as a beacon of light and hope to those around you. Through intentional reflection, goal setting, and action steps, may you cultivate a legacy of positive influence and leave a lasting impact on the lives of others.

Conclusion:

In closing, let us offer a prayer for all men who aspire to be role models in their communities, workplaces, and families.

Heavenly Father, guide us in our journey to become exemplary role models, following the example of your Son, Jesus Christ. Grant us the wisdom, strength, and courage to embody the qualities of speech, conduct, love, faith, and purity outlined in your Word. May our lives be a testament to your grace and goodness, inspiring others to walk in the light of your truth. In Jesus name, Amen.

Chapter 10

Legacy - Leaving a Lasting Impact

"And the things you have heard me say in the presence of many witnesses entrust to reliable people who will also be qualified to teach others."
2 Timothy 2:2

Overview:

As men journey through life, they are often driven by a desire to leave behind a legacy that reflects their values, beliefs, and contributions. In this chapter, we will explore the concept of legacy and discuss practical ways to ensure that our lives have a lasting impact on future generations. Drawing inspiration from 2 Timothy 2:2, we will learn how to entrust valuable teachings to reliable individuals, thereby perpetuating a legacy of wisdom and truth.

In the journey of life, men aspire not only to achieve personal success but also to leave behind a meaningful legacy that outlives them. This desire to make a lasting impact is deeply ingrained in the human spirit, driving men to invest in future generations and sow seeds of wisdom, guidance, and inspiration. Grounded in the timeless wisdom of Scripture, particularly 2 Timothy 2:2, this chapter explores the profound significance of leaving a legacy and provides practical insights on how men can press towards this noble mark.

2 Timothy 2:2 (NIV) - "And the things you have heard me say in the presence of many witnesses entrust to reliable people who will also be qualified to teach others."

This chapter delves into the essence of leaving a legacy and empowers men to embrace their role as stewards of knowledge and virtue.

1. **Qualification to Teach Others:** Before entrusting teachings to others, it is essential to identify individuals who demonstrate reliability, integrity, and a commitment to truth. Those entrusted with the task of teaching others must possess qualities such as faithfulness, competence, and a genuine desire to invest in the lives of others.

2. **Multiplication Effect:** The impact of investing in others extends far beyond the immediate recipients of teachings. Like ripples in a pond, the wisdom passed on to reliable individuals has the potential to multiply exponentially, shaping the lives of countless others and leaving an enduring legacy that spans generations.

3. **Application to Leaving a Legacy:** Applying the principles of 2 Timothy 2:2 to leaving a legacy involves intentional investment in the lives of others, with a focus on passing on timeless truths and values. By identifying reliable individuals, teaching them effectively, and embracing the multiplication effect, men can leave behind a legacy that honors God and blesses future generations.

4. **Teaching Others:** Effective teaching involves more than just imparting knowledge; it requires a heart-to-heart connection and a willingness to lead by example. Men are encouraged to embrace the responsibility of teaching others with clarity, patience, and humility, ensuring that

the lessons they impart are rooted in truth and lived out in their own lives.

As men press towards the mark of leaving a legacy, let us heed the wisdom of Scripture and commit ourselves to the noble task of investing in others. By entrusting teachings to reliable individuals, teaching with integrity and humility, and embracing the multiplication effect, we can leave behind a legacy that echoes through eternity, bringing glory to God and blessing the world.

Reflection Questions:

1. What legacy do you aspire to leave behind?

2. How do your current actions align with the legacy you wish to create?

3. Who are the reliable individuals in your life whom you can entrust with your values and teachings?

Goal Setting:
- ✓ **Define your legacy:** Clearly articulate the values, principles, and contributions you want to be remembered for.

- ✓ **Identify reliable individuals:** Determine who in your life possesses the qualities necessary to carry forward your legacy.

- ✓ **Develop a plan:** Outline specific actions you can take to ensure that your legacy is perpetuated and shared with future generations.

Action Steps:
- **Lead by example:** Live your life by the values and principles you wish to impart to others.

- **Invest in relationships:** Build strong connections with individuals who share your vision and can help carry forward your legacy.

- **Teach and mentor:** Take an active role in passing on your knowledge, wisdom, and experiences to others who can benefit from them.

Journaling Space:

Reflect on your progress towards leaving a legacy:

- What steps have you taken to ensure that your legacy is being perpetuated?

- What challenges have you encountered along the way, and how have you overcome them?

- Write down your thoughts, insights, and aspirations related to leaving a lasting impact on future generations.

CONCLUSION:
KEEP PRESSING TOWARD YOUR MARK!

As we conclude our journey, it's time to reflect on the lessons learned, the growth experienced, and the commitment made to continue pressing towards our marks with renewed purpose and determination. Throughout this book, we've explored various aspects of life where men can strive to make a difference, leaving a lasting impact on their faith, marriages, fatherhood, family, friendships, finances, physical health, careers, role modeling, and legacy. Now, let us take a moment to consolidate our thoughts, reaffirm our commitments, and look forward to the future with hope and resolve.

Reflecting on the Journey:
Take a moment to reflect on your journey through this book. Consider the insights gained, the challenges faced, and the growth experienced in each area of your life. Think about the changes you've made, the goals you've set, and the progress you've achieved. Celebrate your successes, acknowledge your setbacks, and recognize the transformative power of pressing towards your mark.

Commitment to Pressing Towards Your Mark:
As men, our journey towards our mark is ongoing and ever-evolving. It requires dedication, perseverance, and a steadfast commitment to growth. Let this conclusion serve as a reminder of the importance of staying true to ourselves, our values, and our aspirations. Regardless of where you currently stand on your journey, recommit yourself to pressing towards your mark with renewed vigor and determination.

Renewed Purpose and Determination:
As you look ahead to the future, embrace the opportunities that lie before you with renewed

purpose and determination. Remember that each day is a new opportunity to make a difference, to pursue your passions, and to leave a positive impact on the world around you. Whether you're striving to deepen your faith, strengthen your relationships, advance in your career, or leave a lasting legacy, approach each day with intentionality and a sense of purpose.

Continuing the Journey:
While this book may be coming to an end, your journey towards pressing towards your mark is far from over. Let this conclusion serve as a springboard for continued growth, exploration, and self-discovery. Keep seeking knowledge, pursuing excellence, and embracing the challenges and opportunities that come your way. Remember that the mark you're pressing towards is not a destination but a lifelong journey of growth and fulfillment.

Final Thoughts:
As we conclude our time together, I want to express my gratitude for joining me on this journey. It has been a privilege to walk alongside you as we

explored what it means to press toward the mark as men. As you move forward, may you continue to press towards your mark with courage, conviction, and unwavering determination. May your journey be filled with abundant blessings, meaningful relationships, and the fulfillment of your deepest aspirations.

Let us carry its lessons in our hearts and continue pressing towards our mark with courage and conviction. The journey ahead may be challenging, but with faith, perseverance, and a steadfast commitment to growth, we can overcome any obstacle and achieve our greatest aspirations. Here's to pressing towards the mark and living lives of purpose, passion, and fulfillment.

Heavenly Father,
We thank you for the journey we've embarked on together and for the growth and transformation we've experienced along the way. As we conclude this book, we commit ourselves anew to pressing towards our mark with renewed purpose and determination. Guide us, strengthen us, and

empower us to live lives that honor you and bless others. May our journey be a testament to your grace, love, and faithfulness. In Jesus name, we pray. Amen.

Acknowledgments

As I reflect on the journey that has led me to this point, I am filled with gratitude for the countless men who have played a pivotal role in shaping my life and helping me to press toward my mark. It has been a journey spanning over 42 years, marked by challenges, triumphs, and the unwavering support of remarkable individuals who have guided and inspired me along the way.

Childhood:

First and foremost, I owe a debt of gratitude to my father, Fred Quarles Sr., whose love, wisdom, and unwavering support have been a guiding light throughout my life. Alongside him, my brothers Dwayne Quarles Sr., Chris Quarles, Brent Darden, Brandon Flynn, Luther Stroder, Kevin Harrington, Dynel Bailey, and Keith Ellington have been constant sources of strength and inspiration, teaching me the value of resilience and determination.

I am deeply grateful for the influence of my grandfathers, Leslie Grady and George Quarles, whose wisdom and grace have left an indelible mark on my character. In the spiritual realm, Pastor Thomas R. Howard played a significant role in nurturing my faith and instilling in me a sense of purpose and conviction. The camaraderie and fellowship of the Grady & Quarles Men, as well as the men of the Church of the Living God, provided a supportive community where I could grow spiritually and emotionally.

Coach Ken Mitchell was more than just a coach; he was a mentor who taught me the value of discipline, teamwork, and perseverance. And to my teammates at Northwest High School and Pike High School, you were more than just teammates; you were brothers who shared in the journey of growing up and striving for excellence together.

Young Adult:
During my youth and young adult years, I was fortunate to be surrounded by a community of mentors, friends, and colleagues who continued to support and inspire me. My groomsmen stood by my side as I embarked on the journey of marriage, offering their friendship and support. Brothers like Doc Gooden, Chris Pryor, Corey Cobbs, and Riheem Brown were not just friends but pillars of strength and companionship.

The men of the Indiana State Football Team, under the leadership of Coach Tim McGuire, taught me the value of teamwork, discipline, and perseverance.

I am indebted to pastors such as Dr. Keith Norman, Reverend Breckenridge, Nyrone Hawkins, and Keenon Vaughan, whose guidance and spiritual wisdom have been a source of strength and inspiration. Mentors like Mike Arnold and Kem Wilson Jr. provided invaluable counsel and support as I navigated the challenges of young adulthood.

My brothers in faith, including Bryant Henderson, Wendall Jackson, Jerrod Gunter, and Brandon Woodard, have been constant companions on this journey, offering friendship, encouragement, and solidarity in times of need. I am also grateful for the guidance of supervisors like Dr. Luckey, whose mentorship helped me to develop professionally and personally.

<u>Adulthood:</u>
As I transitioned into adulthood, the support and mentorship of family members and trusted advisors continued to shape my path. My father-in-law, Ricky Jackson, and my uncle, Cedric Webster, have been pillars of strength and wisdom, offering invaluable guidance and support.

I am grateful for mentors like Don Mellon, whose insights and counsel have helped me to navigate the complexities of adulthood with grace and resilience. Pastors such as Chris Stull and Greg Brown have been instrumental in deepening my faith and guiding me on my spiritual journey.

To all those whose names may not be mentioned here, please know that your impact on my life has not gone unnoticed or unappreciated. Each of you has played a vital role in helping me to press towards my mark, and for that, I am profoundly grateful.

To every man who has crossed my path, whether mentioned here or not, your presence in my life has been a gift beyond measure, and I am forever grateful for the impact you have had on my journey. As I continue to press towards my mark, I carry with me the lessons, wisdom, and love that you have so generously shared. May we all continue to inspire, uplift, and support one another as we journey through life together.

In closing, I would like to extend my deepest gratitude to every man who has walked alongside me, offered guidance, and helped me to become the person I am today. Your support and encouragement have been invaluable, and I am honored to have journeyed with you as we continue to press towards our marks together.

With heartfelt appreciation,

Fred Quarles Jr.

Made in the USA
Middletown, DE
16 August 2024